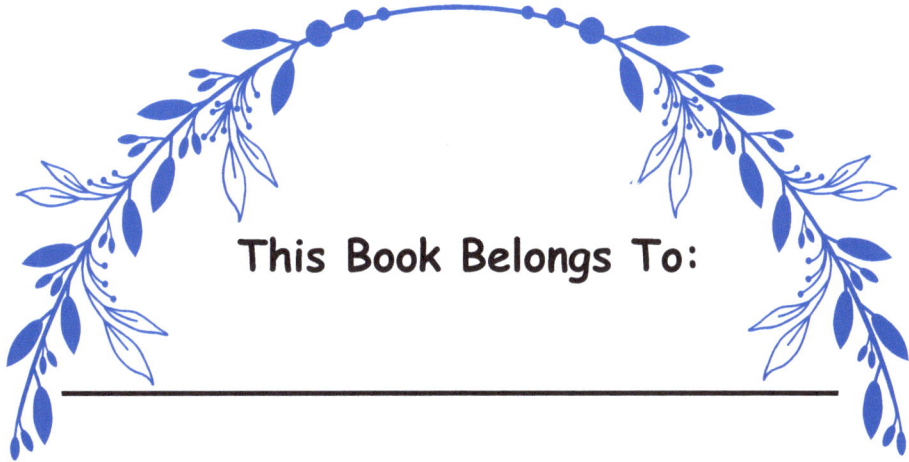

This Book Belongs To:

_____

Presented By:

On:

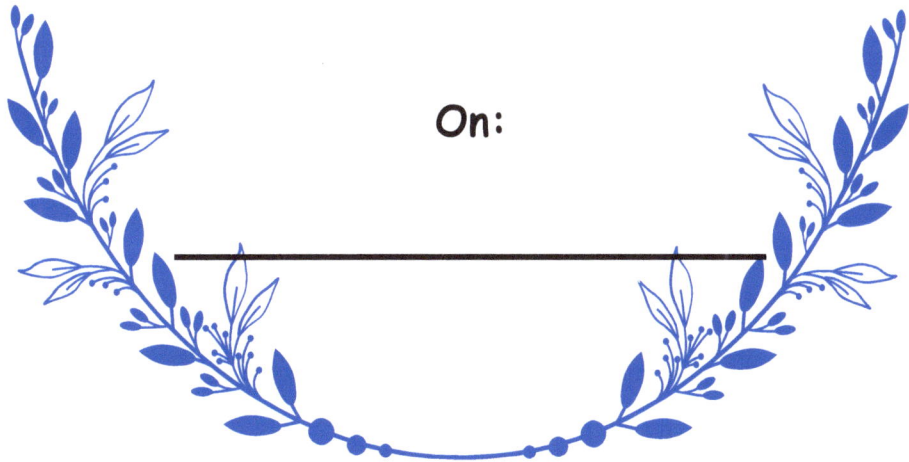

I am graciously dedicating this book to all of my immediate and extended family and friends who reside in the beautiful Great Lakes state of Wisconsin. A wonderful place to grow up. I hope my love for all of you shines through in my writing and my goal is for all of you to own a good collection of my art with this book. God richly bless and keep all of you!

Janice Millane Wasmer also authored these books in this series, "In God's Creation Animals of the Forest", "In God's Creation Animals of the Desert" , "In God's Creation Animals of the Ocean" and "In God's Creation Animals of the Great Plains."

Book design by Janice Millane Wasmer WildArtAmerica Publishing.
Special thanks and appreciation to my two editor-daughters,
Janelle L. Channell and Renaya G. Van Dusen.
Without their loving support, encouragement, and editing this book for me, this endeavor would have been much more difficult.
I would like to acknowledge Photographer Craig Sterken for the use of his photo that I used for reference for the painting on the cover of this book. Craig's photos are available and can be purchased at: CraigSterken.com Thanks Craig!

Another big "Thank You" to my sweet niece Kelli, who helped me choose some of the animal content of this book. Kelli is an avid outdoors and fisher woman who is out almost daily in the Great Lakes region.

Furthermore, I would like to thank my husband, Ed Wasmer, who supports me and my art in every human way possible. To him, I am most grateful.
ISBN 979-8-9907327-7-3 Hardback
www.janicemillanewasmer.com

In God's Creation
Animals of the Great Lakes
A Book for "Kids" of All Ages

Written and Illustrated by Janice Millane Wasmer

So here I go, crazy but true. This is the fifth book in this series of six books. Growing up in Southeastern Wisconsin from my middle school years was quite a neat experience. Our family started in Milwaukee and then moved to the suburbs of Brown Deer when I was probably about 3 years old. We were one of the first houses in the subdivision, and it was one that my Dad designed and built. At the time, finding a house that accommodated 13 people was not easy, so this was one of the big reasons my Dad chose to build it. He contracted out some of the larger jobs, but I remember him doing much of the inside of the house. Mom was only 4'11" tall, so Dad had cabinets and countertops lowered just for her. We all loved that home Mom created. She was efficient in her decorating, never fancy. She was a "no frills" kind of woman.

In 1967, just before I turned 13, Dad moved us to the country—a small rural town. I think he just wanted more open space for us all, and he always loved the outdoors. It was a bit challenging for a few of us due to where we were in our school-age years. It was hard for me because I was in 7th grade going into 8th. We had all gone to the same private school together in Brown Deer. Another one of my sisters had it especially hard because she was entering her Senior year of high school. But, we all adjusted to the move eventually.

In God's Creation
Animals of the Great Lakes
A Book for "Kids" of All Ages

"The heavens tell the glory of God.
And the skies announce what his hands have made."
Psalm 19:1

In the Great Lakes, in God's great creation many creatures thrive. From the tiny midge and firefly to the awesome lake sturgeon, they each have their place and their purpose. God loves them all and will forever provide them abundant food, fresh water, and crispy, clean air. He watches over them with His love and His care.

"The God of gods, the Lord, speaks. He calls the earth from the rising to the setting sun." Psalm 50:1

Two fascinating insects thrive in the dark of night in the Great Lakes region. The firefly you see with its abdomen so bright. While the Midge or "No-See-Um" is a pesky little critter and loves to bite. Midges are an essential food for birds, fish, and other predators. The firefly feeds on pests like slugs and snails and helps to manage the populations of these species. Another adventure awaits in God's Creation. Are you ready to go?

"Let them praise the Lord because they were created by his command." Psalm 148:5

I always wonder when a person says there is no God. How can anyone make such a claim? It never ceases to make me sad. Beautiful, abounding life surrounds us in the magnificent place we call home. And such a comedian God is! Just two nights ago, I watched a documentary on planet Earth. Some of the most crazy and interesting-looking creatures were filmed. Some close-ups looked like my biggest childhood monster fears! They were too funny, amazing, creative, and too creative to not be made by the Great Creator.

"Our Lord and God! You are worthy to receive glory and honor and power. You made all things. Everything existed and was made because you wanted it." Revelation 4:11

In God's beautiful creation, in the lake where water glows, lives a swan that everyone knows. His feathers are white like the softest of clouds, with a voice like a trumpet, he makes us proud. He glides on the surface so smooth and sleek, with a long graceful neck, he's a fancy mystique. A beak the color black, a stylish feature, he's the grandad bird, a faithful nature creature! When the spring arrives with a splash and a cheer. The trumpeter swan brings his family near. Baby cygnets in a fluffy parade swim by his side in the sun and the shade. Come listen, he says, "to my song so grand, I'm a trumpeter swan in this lovely land."

"If a person believes in me, rivers of living water will flow out from his heart. This is what the Scripture says." Psalm 7:38

In God's glorious creation, a river otter slides and glides, his tail all a-swish. He dives so quickly to catch a fish. He is an animal, sleek and spry, as he swims under the bright blue sky. His fur is so dense that it traps the heat. He is built for warmth, which is so neat! On the riverbank, he loves to rest; in his cozy den, his sleep is best. River otters, what a sight! They are nature's joy, pure delight.

"'Jesus said, "Come follow me. I will make you fishermen for men.'"
Matthew 4:19

In God's wonderful creation, lake sturgeons are steadfast and true. They glide through water their whole lives through. With armor-like scales and a whiskered snout, they are mysteries of the lake without any doubt. They are living fossils, as old as time, prehistoric wonders simply sublime. They grow so big, up to eight feet long, in freshwater homes, they live very strong. They sift the lake floor, searching for prey. Snails and worms keep their hunger at bay. Possessing skeletons made of cartilage, not bone, just like sharks in their aquatic home. Gentle giants in the water, so clear, silent protectors we hold so dear.

"He will protect you like a bird spreading its wings over its young. His truth will be like your armor and shield." Psalm 91:4

In God's awesome creation in the sky, vast and blue, snow geese fly a feathery crew. White like snow with black-tipped wings, their honking call the song it brings. They travel far, across the lands, in the cold of winter and summer sands. Together, they will always roam from the Arctic chill to their marshy home. Their V-shaped flight, a wonderful view, and teamwork bound strong and true. Through frosty air and fields, they feed. Snow geese find all that they need. So next time you see them in the bright blue sky. Wave hello as they flutter by!

"So God made the wild animals, the tame animals and all the small crawling animals to produce more of their own kind. God saw that this was good." Genesis 1:25

In God's creative creation, where the tall trees sway, lives a black squirrel who plays all day. With fur so dark, like midnight's hue. A shade that is special and quite unique too. She leaps from branch to branch up high, a daring acrobat beneath the blue sky. Gathering nuts in her fluffy tail, she is a tiny explorer that leaves no trail. While her cousins wear coats of gray or red, this little squirrel with her glossy thread, is an adaptation of nature's art that keeps her warm when the cold winds start. So when you see her along your way, say, "Hello, black squirrel. Have a nutty day!"

"Also, the kingdom of heaven is like a net that was put into the lake. The net caught many different kinds of fish. When it was full, the fishermen pulled the net to the shore. They sat down and put all the good fish in baskets." Mathew 13:47-48

In God's incredible creation, where the water is clear and the sunshine gleams, live two bass cousins who are a lively team. One with a mouth, a modest size, the smallmouth has watchful eyes. He loves the rocks and the currents so strong, a bronzy flash, where he belongs.

The other fish, with a broader grin, is the mighty largemouth, who jumps right in! His jaws extend open and wide, where tasty treats can often hide. In the weedy beds he likes to lurk, a bold hunter with a powerful jerk.

Though they have different mouths, their spirits blend. They are predators, and on chasing minnows, their lives depend. The minnows which are swift and bright. They feel a tug upon the line's tight flight. So next time you fish, remember well the bassy tales the waters tell!

"He satisfies me with good things. He makes me young again, like the eagle." Psalm 103:5

In God's magnificent creation soaring over the shore, an eight-foot wingspan helps this hunter explore. With eyes so keen, they can spot silver fins, where the mighty lakes and wilderness begin. Nesting in the pines, towering and old, they raise their young to be fierce and bold. Nearly lost to pesticides, dark reign, now they flourish by the lakes once again. From Lake Michigan's depths to Erie's waves, these symbols of freedom God's nature saves. Through Lake Huron's mists and Lake Ontario's spray, the Great Lakes Eagle rules each day with strong talons and their vision clear. They fish the waters year after year. It is a victory to celebrate and happily sing as these majestic birds take wing.

"I have given all the green plants to all the animals to eat. They will be food for every wild animal, every bird of the air and every small crawling animal." And it happened." Genesis 1:30

In God's immense creation, a common snapping turtle who is ancient and bold, has lived in the Great Lakes since times very old. With a shell like a tank and jaws mighty strong, she prowls the wetland where she belongs. She doesn't chase fish with a splash and a rush; she waits very still in the water bank brush. Her shell isn't smooth like her pond turtle friends. It's bumpy and ridged, which helps her blend and defend. In the spring, she will dig up dry ground to lay her eggs in a nest she has found. When autumn comes around, tiny turtles emerge, ready for life in the pond's gentle surge. So if by the water you see this old friend. Just watch from afar; let her be in the end. Snappers are guardians of the wetlands, so that is true. Keeping waters healthy for me and you.

"Lord, you have made many things. With your wisdom you made them all. The earth is full of your riches." Psalm 104:24

In God's amazing creation, a little mink with chocolate fur swims so swiftly that he's quite a blur. Semi-webbed paws help him glide. Catching fish by the riverside. From streams to lakes, he loves to roam, making dens his cozy home. He has sharp white teeth and whiskers keen; he's the best swimmer ever seen. Two feet long from nose to tail. On land or water, he never fails. Hunting crawfish, frogs and more, along the peaceful water's shore. All alone, swimming in the night, quick and clever, what a sight! American mink, so free and wild. By land and water, he is nature's child.

"He will protect you like a bird spreading its wings over its young. His truth will be like your armor and shield." Psalm 91:4

In God's bountiful creation on Lake Michigan, Erie, and Superior, too, seagulls soar the skies bright blue. They dance on the waves of the freshwater seas and build their nests high in the trees. In spring, they lay eggs, just three at a time, speckled with brown dots and spots sublime. The chicks are hungry, all fluffy and gray, while mom and dad fish throughout the long day. These smart Great Lakes gulls have figured things out; they drop clams on rocks with a crash and a shout! Breaking the clams wide open, clever birds are these, as they feast on their dinner with natural ease. They don't fly down south in winter like the rest; they stay near the lakes they love the best. Their feathers keep them warm through snow, wind, and rain until springtime brings warm weather again. So wave to these birds when you visit the shores, where the mighty lakes have adventures galore!

"The Lord God gives me my strength. He makes me like a deer, which does not stumble. He leads me safely on the steep mountains."   Habakkuk 3:19

In God's stunning creation with slender legs and gentle eyes, the white-tailed deer leap under the skies. Not quite flying, but leaping high, over the logs and leaves so dry. In a meadow soft and bright, they munch on grass from morning to night. With ears so big and keen to hear, they listen closely for sounds that are near. Their tails are flags so white and bold that they flash up when danger's told. They warn their friends, "Quick, run away! Stay safe, be fast, don't stop and play!" The forest is a cozy home. Through trees and fields, they love to roam. So if you see them standing near, smile and wave to the white-tailed deer!

"Wild birds make nests by the water. They sing among the tree branches." Psalm 104:12

In God's beloved creation in the great blue sky, so wild and free, a red-tailed hawk glides gracefully. Her wings spread wide in the golden sunlight. She rides the wind from morning to night. Her sharp eyes scan both near and far, seeing more than we ever are. A rust-red tail, a feathery crown, she hunts carefully, swooping down. With a high, shrill call, she sings her tune. Over forest, fields, and even dunes. Helping nature, keeping things right, she balances life with silent flight. So if you spot her way up high, watch her dancing across the sky—a fearless flyer, so wild and free. The red-tailed hawk is a sight to see!

"Then Jesus told another story: "The kingdom of heaven is like a mustard seed. A man plants the seed in his field. That seed is the smallest of all seeds. But when it grows, it is one of the largest garden plants. It becomes a tree, big enough for the wild birds to come and make nests in its branches." Matthew 13:31-32

In God's marvelous creation, high above the sparkling water, osprey nest, but they are never a squatter. Their feathers are white and dark like night. Soaring and diving, what a sight! With sharp eyes and talons strong, they hunt for fish the whole day long. Splash! They dive as a hunter, true, scoop their dinner, and off they flew. Their nest is so high on a sturdy tree, home to little chicks they care for with ease. Mom and Dad bring them food and keep them safe in a caring mood. Osprey glide where rivers flow and where the breezy currents blow. A fisherbird so bold and bright. They rule the skies from morning light!

"I love you, Lord. You are my strength. The Lord is my rock, my protection, my Savior. My God is my rock. I can run to him for safety. He is my shield and my saving strength, my high tower."
Psalm 18:1-2

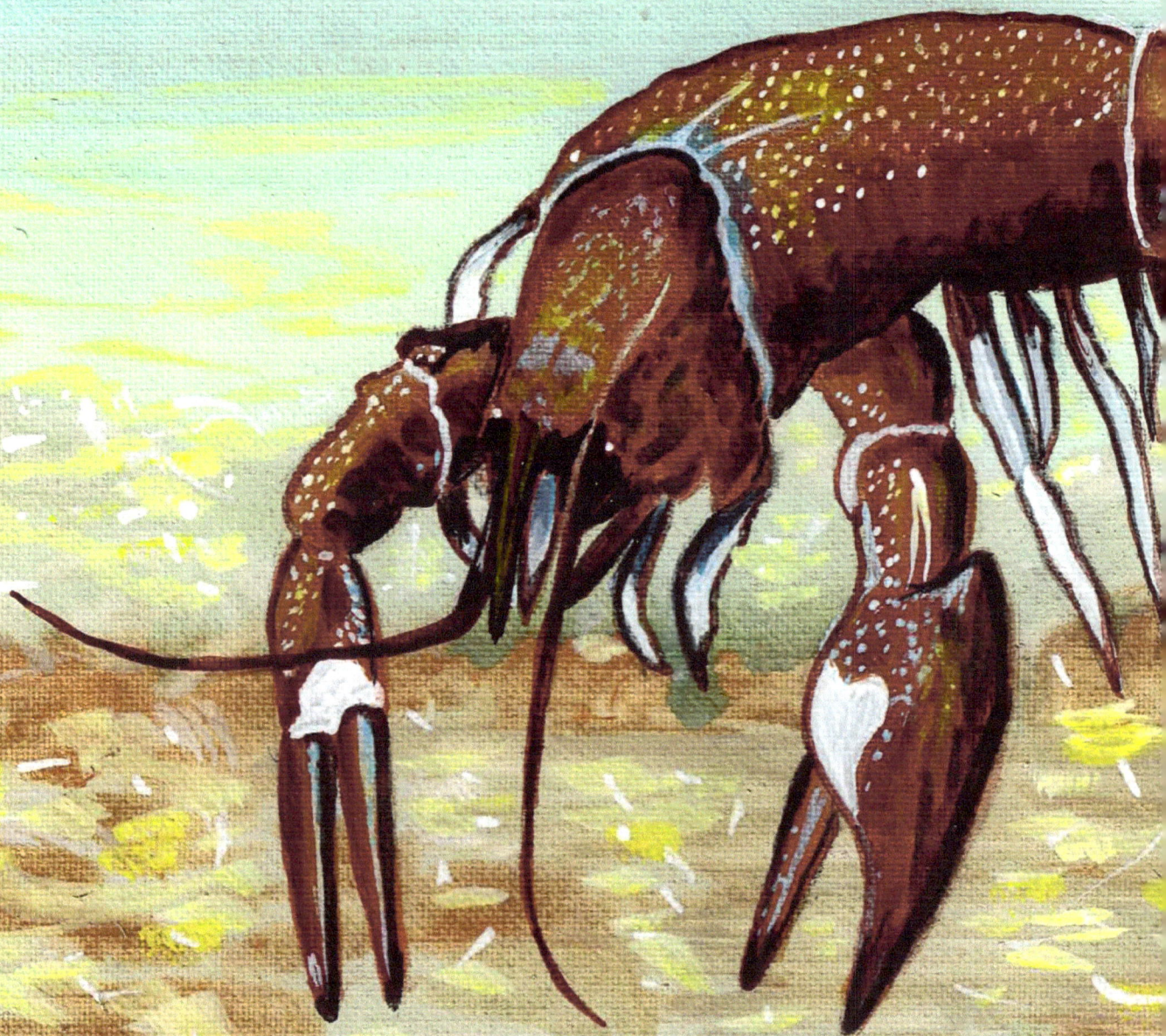

In God's brilliant creation, where the waters flow, lives a little crawfish; watch her go! Rusty crawfish are small and bright. She scuttles left and scuttles right! With her claws so big and wide, she waves hello, then runs to hide. Once she lived in waters small, now she travels one and all! Spreading far, she makes her way, changing rivers day by day. So if you see her scuttle near, remember she's a pioneer! Rusty crawfish, bold and free, where will your next adventure be?

"Look at the birds in the air. They don't plant or harvest or store food in barns. But your heavenly Father feeds the birds. And you know that you are worth much more than the birds."
Matthew 6:26

In God's excellent creation out on the lake at the break of day, loons are calling, "Yoo Hoo! Hooray!" Their eerie cry floats through the air, a wild sound beyond compare. With striking eyes, red like a glow, speckled feathers white on black rows. They seem so smooth-no rush-no race, then they vanish without a trace! Down they dive like a feathered fish, to catch a meal, a tasty dish. A slippery snack, wiggling fast, but loons are quick to capture them at last! Loon's wings are built for flight so high, and though on land, they are not very spry. They soar for miles, tried and true, to find a lake both brilliant and blue. So listen closely when the loons call loud; their laughing song is so very proud. A bird so wild, both strange and bright, a treasure of the Great Lakes night.

"When Jesus had finished speaking, He said to Simon, "Take the boat into deep water. If you will put your nets in the water, you will catch some fish." Luke 5:4

In God's majestic creation, down in the lake where the waters flow, lives a sneaky fish you might not know. She has golden scales that gleam and glow. Her staring eyes steal the show! The walleye pike with her wiggle-ZIP! Zap! Zoom! She catches a snack and seals its doom. She blinks one eye, playing it cool, pretending to nap the trickster's tool! But when a minnow swims too near, the walleye grins, "Come here, my dear!" Though big and bold, she makes no fuss unless she meets a fisherman's truss. So if you see her flashing tail, so swift, so sly, this wily walleye is waving goodbye!

"So if the Son makes you free, then you will be truly free." John 8:36.

In God's powerful creation, in the marsh where waters flow, stands a heron; he is calm and slow. With his blue feathers, he is so long and tall. The Great Blue Heron is the king of them all. He wades through the reeds with a graceful stride on a quest for fish that swim and glide. With a sharp, long beak that's quick and keen, he catches his dinner--a true fishing machine! His legs are like stilts; he is a sight to see beside a pond or a big oak tree. He spreads his wings; oh, what a show! A canvas of blue against skies aglow. When the sun is low and the day is done, he returns to his nest, a day well-run. With beauty and grace, he lives life free. A wonderful bird for you and me!

"Every animal on earth and every bird in the sky will respect and fear you. So will every animal that crawls on the ground and every fish in the sea respect and fear you. I have given them to you."
Genesis 9:2

In God's astounding creation, up in a tall tree that sways, lives a creature who is quite shy all her days. With a wiggly nose and big bright eyes, the porcupine scurries, oh, what a surprise! Covered in quills that are sharp as a pin, when danger is near, that's where it begins. She puffs up her spines, looking quite tough, but really, she is gentle and pretty sweet stuff. Eating leaves and bark and any fruit she can find, this porcupine munches, so calm and so kind. In the moonlight, she will roam and explore—solitary friends, never a bore. So if you see one, give a cheer, for this prickly creature is special, my dear!

"Then God said, 'Let us make human beings in our image and likeness. And let them rule over the fish in the sea and the birds in the sky. Let them rule over the tame animals, over all the earth and over all the small crawling animals on the earth.'" Genesis 1:26

In God's splendorous creation in the crystal lake where the tall pines sway, fishes called Muskie are so bold and gray. With stripes like a tiger and a smile so wide, they glide through the water, a true lake guide. With fins that are strong and a body so sleek, they hide in shadows, so crafty, unique. Hunters of fish, they are swift and sly. With a flick of their tails, they zip on by! They are the rulers of the lake. In their watery home. Where lily pads float and dragonflies roam. Though they seem fierce, they are gentle at heart. Just out for a swim--a true work of art. So, if you are fishing on a bright summer day, watch for the Muskie in the shimmering spray. They are creatures, so magic, sleek and grand. A symbol of nature in this beautiful land!

"My God will use his wonderful riches in Christ Jesus to give you everything you need." Philippians 4:19

In God's blessed creation, where the grass is green or gold, lives the wild turkey with his stories to be told. He struts and flaps with a cheer, the funniest bird you will ever hear! He makes a silly honking sound, spreading joy all around. His gobble echoes through the trees while he dances and plays in the autumn leaves. With feathers brown, gold, and red, he has a wattle on his head. When it's chilly, he puffs up wide to keep him warm in winter's countryside. On Thanksgiving, he had better run because hunters are not out just for fun—a meal he will make on this special day. So run, Mr. Turkey, so that you can live another day!

In God's divine creation, in the gentle dawn's embrace, the sun begins to rise. God paints the heavens with colors so wise. Each flower that blooms, each tree standing tall, His whispers of love echo through all. The stars in the sky, like diamonds, gleam. Each one is a reminder of His love's boundless dream. The vastness of the Great Lakes and the grace of the breeze, all crafted with care, to bring hearts to peace. He formed every creature, both great and small. With His purpose and beauty, He loves them all. From the tiniest of fireflies to the mightiest deer, each life is a story and brings us such cheer. In the stillness of night, through the day's radiant glow, His love weaves a tapestry of so much more than we know. In every heartbeat, in every sigh, we're all part of his masterpiece under the sky.

But as it is written in the Scriptures: "No one has ever seen this. No one has ever heard about it. No one as ever imagined what God has prepared for those who love him." 1 Corinthians 2:9

It never ends for those who love Him!

www.ingramcontent.com/pod-product-compliance
Lightning Source LLC
Chambersburg PA
CBHW041548260326
41914CB00016B/1586